The Distracted Dance of Resilience

The Distracted Dance of Resilience

DANCING AWAY FROM LIFE'S HURTS
TOWARDS HEALING AND RESTORATION

Katina J. Boyd

Dedication

To my phenomenal daughters whom I love dearly and are living illustrations of resilience...thank you for being so understanding on my path towards healing. I have been blessed by your support, mommy-makeovers, and love.

To my husband, Jeff, thank you for being my pillar of calmness and love.

To my mother, thank you for ALWAYS being my strongest supporter.

To Braxton, my "bonus baby", thank you for your love and respect.

To the radiant souls reading this book—the heartbroken, betrayed, rejected, not chosen, in-between, or disappointed—I have been right where you are. You are NOT alone. God sees you and He cares about your life. My prayer for you is that you become empowered with resilience and peace as you "spiritually dance" through this devotional.

Table of Contents

Introduction

"Everybody has a plan until you get punched in the mouth."

— MIKE TYSON

HAVE YOU EVER FELT LIKE rejection, heartbreak or betrayal punched you in the mouth?

Me too.

My ex-husband's serial infidelity and our eventual divorce punched me in the mouth so hard...I saw stars. Stunned and fear-gazed, I staggered around the ring of my life throwing wild unsuccessful punches against the body blows of rejection.

Divorce was not part of the dream I had for my life and I got punch-drunk trying to battle disappointment, anger, loneliness, rage, and embarrassment.

I'm a dancer, not a fighter.

God distracted me away from my problems by leading me in some "spiritual dance steps" towards His way of healing and restoration.

I call our duet The Distracted Dance of Resilience. The Distracted Dance of Resilience is a beautiful surrender of what you hoped would have happened.

The "spiritual dance steps" God prompted me to take helped me:

* Shake off the bitterness of heartbreak
* Move on with my life
* Tell my story healthy and whole.

Although my punch was divorce, rejection does not discriminate. The loss of a job, not getting into a school or program, being betrayed by a friend or many other circumstances can leave you emotionally stagger-ing in pain just like you were punched square in your mouth.

If letting go of bitterness, moving on with your life, and helping others by telling your story is of interest to you, this twenty-one day devotional and the power of the Holy Spirit will help you begin the process of healing. I have outlined seven major concepts God impressed upon my heart and included three days of devotions for each concept. Spiritual "dance step" activities are listed at the end of each day's devotion.

As a disclaimer, the words poured out on these pages do not promote divorce. Preserving a marriage with two people invested in reconciliation is incredible and worth the struggle. In addition, the purpose of this devotional is not to bash my ex-husband. He is a great father to our girls and I wish him nothing but light and love.

I certainly do NOT have it all figured out. But, I am the poster child that proves Joel 2:25 is true when God says: "I will repay you for the years the locusts have eaten."

It didn't happen all at once but everything taken from me—God replaced. I am happily remarried, finally comfortable in my own skin, accept my part in the demise of my first marriage and I am able to effectively co-parent with my ex-husband.

Spend the next twenty-one days dancing your way towards flexibility, balance, confidence and ultimately, resilience by reading my struggles and lessons learned.

Are you ready to bounce back better than ever?
Let's go!

Trust God's Character

WHEN I WAS A LITTLE girl, my Daddy spent a lot of time talking to me about "how the world works." At five years old, I already knew the popular phrase…"your word is your bond." I also knew if your "word" couldn't be trusted—you couldn't be trusted.

Perhaps my upbringing is one of the reasons betrayal and infidelity hit me so forcefully. Words were spoken but not fulfilled. Promises were made then eventually broken. Those unfulfilled words and broken promises were heavy, difficult to process, and were two critical ingredients in the "cynical pie" I began to bake.

Out of my disappointment and fear, I became skeptical, doubtful, distrustful, suspicious, and disbelieving about men particularly—but also about new opportunities and the direction of my life.

Divorce was not what I planned and there was nothing I could do to reverse the affairs or make my life like what I dreamed it would be.

So, I smiled on the outside, but I cynically snarled on the inside and became numb.

"Cynicism protects you from crushing disappointment but paralyzes you from doing anything." (Paul Miller *A Praying Life*)

In those first few weeks after I learned of my ex-husband's last affair, paralyzed would be an understatement. I was fixated on what he was doing, the state of our marriage, the hurt of it all, I was not happy on my job, and I felt stupid.

Very well meaning people told me, "You will just have to trust God." Oooookay, thanks I feel better now (not).

What people didn't understand was my world was ROCKED and there were times when I thought I would die from a broken heart. Although I knew the advice to trust God was sound, I couldn't figure out how to wake up one day and do it.

When you are cynical, optimism is not the cure. (At least it wasn't for me.)

I was too down to be optimistic or faithful.

I also felt guilty about feeling the way I did. I led Bible studies so why couldn't I be sincerely optimistic? I was on the greeter team and hosted Christian fitness classes, why couldn't I muster up some hope? Where was my faith?

My faith was not missing….it was misplaced. I put my faith in my marriage, ex-husband, and our family.

I knew I needed to trust God, but it's tough to trust someone you don't know.

Before I could take the advice to "trust God," I had to get to know Him.

So I got "distracted" from all the foolishness of my life into dancing towards understanding who God is.

I began to consistently spend time with God in prayer and reading His Word. A friend suggested I read Bible verses about God's character. Learning about the attributes of God helped me begin to trust Him. My ears had processed so many lies it was like a soothing lullaby to read:

God is not human, that he should lie, not a human being, that he should change his mind. Does he speak and then not act? Does he promise and not fulfill? (Numbers 23:19 NIV)

When I thought about it, I realized, God had NEVER promised me anything He didn't fulfill.

In realizing God kept His promises and was truthful, I was finally able to be honest in my prayer time.

One day, I got in my car, went for a drive (so my children would not hear me), and I screamed/prayed to God about the status of things in my life. I did not sugar coat anything or use kind words.

If God could be trusted, I was going to start by "keeping it 100." I didn't feel faithful, hopeful, or loving and I laid all my cynical feelings right out on my dashboard.

After crying, yelling, and pounding my steering wheel for about fifteen minutes, quietness caused me to pause and look around. There was nothing there. The first words that came to my mind were: "Thank you, Katina. I can work with that."

Wait a minute! Who said that?

I believe it was God speaking to me.

If God said He could work with all I had just spewed to Him including the F-bomb I'm pretty sure I dropped...I had to know more about Him.

Here are a few of the first verses I studied about God's character:

God is powerful (Omnipotent)

"Behold, I am the Lord, the God of all flesh. Is anything too hard for me? Jeremiah 32:27 (ESV)

God is faithful

Know therefore that the LORD your God is God; he is the faithful God, keeping his covenant of love to a thousand generations of those who love him and keep his commands.– Deuteronomy 7:9 (ESV)

God is just

The Rock! His work is perfect, For all His ways are justice. A God of faithfulness and without iniquity, just upright is He." – Deuteronomy 32:4 (ESV)

God does not change

"For I the Lord do not change; therefore you, O children of Jacob are not consumed. Malachi 3:6 (ESV)

God is loving

But God shows his love for us in that while we were still sinners, Christ died for us. Romans 5:8 (ESV)

God is wise

Oh, the depth of the riches both of the wisdom and knowledge of God! How unsearchable are His judgments and unfathomable His ways! Romans 11:33 (ESV)

God is omnipresent (He is everywhere)

"Am I a God at hand, declares the Lord and not a God far away? Can a man hide himself in secret places so I cannot see him? declares the Lord. Do I not fill heaven and earth? Declares the Lord. Jeremiah 23:23-24 (ESV)

When you know God is always present, all knowledgeable, all-powerful, loving, just, merciful and good….it becomes easier to trust HIM with an unknown future.

Just like ballet is the foundation of all other dance formats, trusting God is the foundation of the Dance of Resilience.

Which one of the verses shared about God's character spoke to you the most?

Prayer:

Dear God,

Thank you for never changing, being all knowing and all-powerful. Forgive us for not trusting You as we should. Please help us remember to trust You instead of figuring things out on our own.

Amen

Dance Step:

Pull out an index card, write the following sentence and fill in the blanks:

Lord I trust you with _____. I don't know what the future holds but I know you are _____, _____, _____.

Post the index card on your bathroom mirror or any other place you will see it daily.

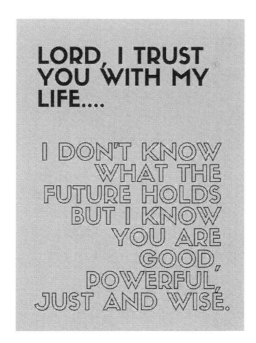

Trust God's Track Record

ONE WORRY-FILLED, TEAR STAINED FACE morning, I texted my friend Nichole. Honestly, I had so much going on, I'm not sure what I texted her about but I will never forget her response. She responded... "Trust God's Track Record."

She didn't have any specific instructions about my problem. However, her text caused me to pause, take a breath, and reflect.

What was God's track record? Light bulb moment...He is and was UNDEFEATED!

When I looked back at my life, I could only shake my head. How could I forget all the things God brought me through? How could I not remember the things He restored and replaced in my life and the people He provided to comfort me at my lowest moments?

Have you ever forgotten how God brought you through?

How could we forget?

We forget because we focus on the problem.

We must get "distracted" into remembering how God brought us through in the past and allow our past victories to give us hope for today.

Although it offers a seemingly simplified answer to serious heartache and pain, remembering what God has done is powerful and provides comfort.

But this I call to mind, and therefore I have hope: The steadfast love of the Lord never ceases; his mercies never come to

an end; they are new every morning; great is your faithfulness. Lamentations 3:21-22 ESV

In some of my lowest moments journeying through my divorce, I felt like I was going to die. I felt destroyed...but God! I lived, and if you're reading this, you did too!

We are afflicted in every way, but not crushed; perplexed, but not driven to despair, persecuted, but not forsaken; struck down but not destroyed. 2 Corinthians 4:8-9 ESV

Although it feels like it, this betrayal, hurt, rejection or loss will not take you out.

Make Nichole's text (Trust God's Track Record) a mantra for your life.

When the bitter sting of rejection or the pain of unmet expectations remind you something is wrong....remember to trust God's track record.

What is God's track record in your life?

Prayer:

Dear God,

Thank you for being an amazing Heavenly Father who has an undefeated track record. We can always depend on you especially when people let us down. Help us remember all of Your good works when things do not work out like we wanted. We praise You and we trust Your track record.

Amen

Dance step:

1. Look back over your life and write down one situation God brought you through.

_____

_____

_____

_____

_____

_____

_____

_____

_____

_____

_____

_____

_____

_____

_____

_____

_____

_____

_____

_____

_____

_____

_____

_____

_____

_____

_____

_____

Trust God—Don't Forget

YESTERDAY, WE TALKED ABOUT REMEMBERING God's goodness and how He delivered us in the past. Remembering seems so simplistic when we are hurting and feel like there must be something else we can do. When we fly off into action "doing something else," we forget.

Forgetting how God delivered us in the past decreases our faith, causes rebellion and leads to unwise decisions.

Psalm 106:7 reads: "they did not remember the abundance of your steadfast love, but rebelled by the sea, at the Red Sea." (ESV)

"They" in the previous text were the Israelites who were JUST brought out of slavery (a miracle) but when faced with an obstacle (the Red Sea), became ungrateful.

Finally after watching the Red Sea part, walking to safety, and seeing their enemies being swallowed by the same water… they believed!

But they soon forgot his works; they did not wait for his counsel. Psalm 106:13 ESV

A mere three days after watching the miracle of the Red Sea, the Israelites began to complain about not having enough water (Exodus

15:24). They almost immediately forgot about God's power and goodness towards them and did not believe He could help them.

When they forgot about what God did, they became impulsive. We must trust God's track record and wait for His plan to unfold.

Trusting and waiting seem like weaknesses in today's culture. Gorgeous, influential people on every TV network and social media platform model making "now" decisions for us every day.

Unfortunately, the fallout of those "now decisions" does not pull ratings or followers.

But it wasn't long before they forgot the whole thing, wouldn't wait to be told what to do. The Israelites only cared about pleasing themselves in that desert, provoked God with their insistent demands. (Psalm 106: 13-14 The Message)

The Israelites forgot what God did for them. They complained when they did not have water, gossiped about not having food, got bored with the food God provided (manna) and demanded meat.

They wouldn't just trust God's PROVEN track record and wait.

And because they wouldn't…

Psalm 106:15
He gave them exactly what they asked for—but along with it, they got an empty heart. (The Message)

The Israelites wanted and demanded meat, so God provided flocks of quails for them. After eating freely of the quails for a full month, the food became "loathsome" (disgusting, repulsive) to them. (Numbers 11:20)

They forgot, complained, made crazy requests because they thought they knew what they wanted at the moment but ended up feeling repulsive.

That is the world's way, and if we are all honest, we have all been in that cycle.

This time, we are NOT going to focus on our fearful instincts that lead us astray.

This time, we are going to get distracted with memories of how God delivered us in the past. If He did it before, He will do it again.

I have made Nichole's text a mantra for my life. When things happen, I begin to say over and over... Trust God's Track Record.

In Psalm 103:2 David told himself to never forget the good things God has done. We also must make up our minds to never forget God's goodness in our lives.

Prayer:

Dear God,

Thank you for bringing us through so many times in our lives. We know you protect us and care for us when we are not even aware of your presence. Help us to not get so distracted with our problems that we forget how you have comforted us and handled our situations in the past.

Amen

Dance Step

Begin to journal your struggle and prayers then go back and read them at a later date. (You will be amazed at how God came through for you!)

Self Care-Rest

IN MY OPINION THE OLD saying "time heals all wounds" is not true. As I was going through my divorce, people often told me "you just need more time." As if just by weeks or years going by I would magically "glow up" and "live my best life."

Some days, waiting seemed ok. Other days, I wanted to do something. Culture supported me either way. While some people said to wait and feel better other people told me: "Girl, the best way to get over one man is to get up under another one."

Thankfully, God called me into a different distraction. When everything was uncertain, messy, super painful, and instigating, God called me to return to Him and rest.

For thus said the Lord GOD, the Holy One of Israel, "In returning and rest you shall be saved in quietness and in trust shall be your strength." Isaiah 30:15 ESV

Returning in this context means repentance. The Oxford English Dictionary defines repentance as: To review one's actions and feel contrition (remorse) or regret for something one has done or omitted to do; (esp. in religious contexts) to acknowledge the sinfulness of one's past action or conduct by showing sincere remorse and undertaking to reform in the future.

I had to ask myself, what was my part in the breakdown of my marriage? What things or activities was I allowing in my life or participating in that did not line up to God's standard?

With God's help, what did I need to change about me?

Wait a minute. Wasn't I the one hurt?

YES.

But it is not about the offender.

It is about God and me.

It is about God and you.

What is your part in your situation?

Return and rest are all about self-reflection and finding peace in God's comfort by taking our concerns to Him through prayer, solitude, quiet, walking in nature or other spirit led activities. Returning and resting is true Self Care.

God, the Master, The Holy of Israel, has this solemn counsel: "Your salvation requires you to turn back to me—and stop your silly efforts to save yourselves. Your strength will come from settling down in complete dependence on me—The very thing you've been unwilling to do. Isaiah 30:15 (The Message)

Wow. Our strength is in settling down and quietly trusting God...but we are unwilling!

It is so tempting to go everywhere, see and hear everything, and gain every experience. Seeking our own answers, looking for fulfillment from a new job, new love interest or activities, and telling anyone who will listen all about our hurt will not get us any closer to being healed.

So, we have a choice.

Return and rest or: worry, ruminate, escape into things not good for us, and become frustrated, overwhelmed, and bitter.

If returning and resting sound effortless...it's because they are. We can return and enter God's rest by grace. We don't have to perform.

Jesus made this possible when He gave up His life and took the guilt, shame, and condemnation of our sin upon himself. Jesus is how we access God's grace so we can rest.

Prayer:
Lord please forgive us for being unwilling to do things Your way. Thank you for always being there to comfort and save us after we have exhausted ourselves trying everything else to bring us peace. Amen

Have you accepted Jesus as your personal Lord and Savior?

Dance Step(s):
If you have not accepted Jesus as your personal Lord and Savior, there is no time better than right now! Romans 10:19 promises, "if you confess with your mouth that Jesus is Lord and believe in your heart that God raised him from the dead, you will be saved." ESV

Say the following Prayer:

"Dear God, I realize I am a sinner and could never reach heaven by my own good deeds. Right now I place my faith in Jesus Christ as God's Son who lived a perfect life, died for my sins, and rose from the dead to give me eternal life. Please forgive me of my sins and bring me into right relationship with you. Thank you for accepting me and giving me eternal life."
Amen

Send me an email to katinajboyd@gmail.com. I would love to pray for you and discuss next steps.

If you have already accepted Jesus as your personal Lord and Savior:
Turn on some slow worship music and sit on the floor with your legs crossed (if you can). Place your arms on your thighs with your palms up. Close your eyes and ask God to reveal your part in your hurt to you and what your next steps should be.

Need song suggestions? My favorites: O Come to the Altar Acoustic (Elevation Worship), Holy Spirit (Francesca Battistelli), Yahweh Acoustic (Elevation Worship), Turning Around For Me (VaShawn Mitchell) Oceans (Christafari)

Write down any revelations.

Self Care-Solitude

As THE DAYS AND WEEKS passed during my separation, I began to get super fidgety during my morning "quiet time." I put quiet time in quotations because my morning devotion time was usually not quiet. I often played worship music in the background and did a lot of talking to God. When my mornings got hurried, I spent my "quiet time" listening to a sermon from one of my favorite pastors, as I got ready. Silence felt awkward and harsh.

Can you imagine the dramatic eye roll I wanted to perform when a friend suggested I begin to meditate? "Just clear your mind," she said.

Clear my mind? Impossible! I tried to meditate and let me tell you, my brain got a gold medal in "mental gymnastics." As soon as I sat down and cut everything off, my mind took off running and did the pole vault.

One morning, I couldn't get a podcast of a sermon to play and just as I went to put on some worship music, I felt led to get ready in silence. (GASP!) As soon as I could hear the hum of my air conditioner, thoughts crowded my mind. I was too weary to try to "clear my mind" so I just let the opinions, ideas, and theories fly.

Some of those thoughts were not pretty. But when I let them "be," the thoughts only stung for a moment. Although I didn't feel like anything "happened" during my quiet time, I kept sitting quietly in the mornings.

While I sat morning after morning thinking nothing was happening, God was distracting me away from trying to solve my problems into simply bringing my thoughts and concerns to Him.

Lamentations 3: 28-30 instructs us this way:
When life is heavy and hard to take, go off by yourself. Enter
the silence. Bow in prayer. Don't ask questions: Wait for hope to
appear. Don't run from trouble. Take it full-face. The "worst"
is never the worst. (The Message)

Wow.
Enter the silence
Don't ask questions.
Wait for hope to appear.
Don't run from trouble.
Take it full face.
The worst is never the worst.
Why? **Because the Master won't ever walk out and fail to return.**
Lamentations 3:31 (The Message)

God instructs us to stop running into busyness and the noise of life
to get away from our troubles and invites us to enter the silence and
wait for hope to appear. Facing the ugly truth of our situation seems too
painful to bear. So, we call a friend or surf the Internet instead.

God's Word instructs us to look trouble straight in the eye and take
the punch.

Feel the sting and numbness as your bottom lip swells from the blow.

Taste the salty tears as they stream down your face.

Climb into your Heavenly Father's lap in quiet submission and be
comforted.

People may walk out on us, not choose us, or lie to our faces, but
God will always be with us.

Open the gift of solitude today.

Prayer

Dear God,

Thank you for the gift of quiet and solitude. Forgive me for not accepting your gift and making a habit of trying to avoid my issues. Please help me remember where my strength comes from and that You are always with me.

Amen

Dance Steps:

1. Find a quiet place in your home where you can spend five to ten minutes in complete silence (no electronics, music, singing, or talking).

2. Write down how you felt during your quiet time.

_____
_____
_____
_____
_____
_____
_____
_____

3. Write down any revelations you felt during your quiet time.

_____
_____
_____
_____
_____
_____
_____
_____

Self Care-Delegate

WHEN I WAS A "NEW" single mom, I was determined to do it all. I mean, I wasn't the first woman to run a single household nor would I be the last…right? If I could have figured out a realistic way to split myself in two and be everywhere, I would have done it. Annnnnd, since we are being honest…I tried really hard and failed. I was exhausted emotionally and physically. I didn't want to burden anyone with my stuff, so I stiffened my upper lip and did what needed to be done and then some.

The only problem with my stiff upper lipping and pulling myself up by the bootstraps is that I was ridiculously irritable and snappy (especially to my girls—the very people I cared the most about).

One day, I finagled a way to get my hair done. As my stylist draped the warm cape around me, I melted into the chair and became a puddle of tears when she asked the standard question, "So what are we doing today?"

Of course, she was talking about what were we going to do with my hair. I was thinking about all the other stuff I needed to get done.

My stylist placed her hands on my shoulders and looked me right in my eyes through the massive mirror on her workstation and said, "You cannot keep doing everything by yourself. You are going to have to delegate some things to other people."

Her words were actually the same God-inspired leadership advice Moses received from his father-in-law when he saw all the things Moses was doing for the Israelites:

Moses' father-in-law said to him, "What you are doing is not good. You and the people with you will certainly wear yourselves out, for the thing is too heavy for you. You are not able to do it alone. (Exodus 18:17-18) ESV

Since my mini-breakdown in my stylist's chair, God has distracted me from attempting to be Super Girl many times by placing these three words in my spirit: "use your resources."

It was difficult at first, but I learned how to rely on "other capable people," and I motivated my daughters to take on more household responsibilities.

Allowing other people to lighten our load while we process is a huge step in the path to healing. Taking care of ourselves may mean we need to seek the professional help of a counselor or therapist. I am very thankful for my therapist. There is no shame in seeking and accepting help.

Who are your capable people?

How can you use your resources?

"Sometimes self-care means stepping away and graciously allowing others to help us with our burdens." – Cindy Hess Kasper

Prayer:

Dear Lord,

Thank you for your love, comfort, and care. Forgive me for the many times I decided to do it all on my own. Please energize my spirit and enable me to bring balance to my life. Help me recognize and use my resources appropriately.

Amen

Dance Steps:

1. Make a list of capable people you can call on to help you.

_____

_____

_____

_____

_____

_____

_____

_____

2. Ask those people in advance if they would be willing to help and determine how to involve them.

3. Could you share responsibilities with someone on your list? (Carpool, errands, childcare swapping, etc.)

_____

_____

_____

_____

_____

_____

_____

_____

Stockdale Paradox-Faith

I WILL NEVER FORGET THE day my old boss called me into his office "to talk." After about two minutes of pleasantries, he began to tell me how he was planning some restructuring, and he wanted to keep me in the loop. The new pharmacist I trained would be taking my leadership position, and I would now answer to him. Although there was no pay decrease, it felt like I got kicked in the stomach while I was already down.

I listened intently to my boss while smiling and nodding. He asked me if I had any questions and I nodded no. I got up from the chair and left his office the way you rush to the bathroom when you have waited too long and really need to go. I went to my car. Just after closing the door, I burst into tears.

I sobbed. I was heartbroken and I felt stupid. In all honesty, the other pharmacist was a better fit for the leadership position. (Geez that was tough to admit). I was in the middle of my divorce, and I felt like I was failing in every area of my life. I knew God was able to change my situation but what if He didn't?

I wish I could tell you I got the answer to my question as I wiped my tears sitting in my car, but I didn't. Actually, God revealed the answer a few years later when I read the iconic business book *Good to Great* by Jim Collins. In the book, Collins presents a business concept called the Stockdale Paradox.

The Stockdale Paradox is named after Jim Stockdale who was an American Naval Pilot in the Vietnam War. Stockdale was captured and became a POW (prisoner of war). He spent eight gruesome years in a war camp in Vietnam. Although tortured more than twenty times, Stockdale developed a tapping system to communicate with other prisoners while in solitary confinement and became a source of encouragement.

After he was able to escape, he explained how he survived:

"I never doubted not only that I would get out, but also that I would prevail in the end and turn the experience into the defining event of my life, which, in retrospect, I would not trade."

Then comes the paradox:

"You must retain faith that you will prevail in the end, regardless of the difficulties.

AND at the same time, you must confront the most brutal facts of your current reality, whatever they might be."

Interestingly, Admiral Stockdale said "the optimists" were the first to die:

"They were the ones who said, 'We're going to be out by Christmas.' And Christmas would come, and Christmas would go. Then they'd say, 'We're going to be out by Easter.' And Easter would come, and Easter would go. And then Thanksgiving, and then it would be Christmas again. And they died of a broken heart."

Smack dab in the middle of a business book teaching companies how to move from good to great, God showed me a life management system.

We must retain faith that (with God) we will prevail yet we must also confront the brutal facts of our current reality.

In the Bible, the familiar story of the three Hebrew Boys - Shadrach, Meshach and Abednego demonstrates the Stockdale Paradox amazingly.

Although I have read the story of the three Hebrew boys dozens of times, I missed their declaration of faith in the midst of accepting the gravity of their situation.

The King of the land, King Nebuchadnezzar, erected a gold image and commanded the people to bow down to the image. The King was furious when he heard the boys would not follow his command and he gave them an ultimatum:

> **...But if you do not worship, you shall be cast immediately into the midst of a burning fiery furnace. And who is the god who will deliver you from my hands?" Shadrach, Meshach, and Abed-Nego answered and said to the king, "O Nebuchadnezzar, we have no need to answer you in this matter. If that is the case, our God whom we serve is able to deliver us from the burning fiery furnace, and He will deliver us from your hand, O king. But if not, let it be known to you, O king, that we do not serve your gods, nor will we worship the gold image which you have set up." (Daniel 3:16-18 ESV)**

The Hebrew boys delivered a proclamation that serves as a platform to stand on when the storms of life attempt to uproot our peace, comfort, and hope.

The boys proclaimed:

1. "Our God...is able to deliver us."
2. "He will deliver us"
   And then the paradox...
3. "But if not ..."

Those three simple words, "But if not" are the life management system of faith.

God is able and He will but even if He doesn't....

- We know He is working things out for our good. (Romans 8:28 ESV)
- We can muster the courage to do the things we need to do because He is always with us. (Joshua 1:9 ESV)
- We can face the harsh reality of what is because He has conquered the world. (John 16:33 ESV)

Over time, God has taught me to stop focusing on the results and become distracted with "But if not." When I proclaim "But if not," I leave the results up to God. When I say "But if not," I relinquish attachment to my desires and dreams. When I say "But if not," I exercise my faith.

A well-managed life includes "But if not" as part of the process yet couples it with a knowing all will be WELL.

Now faith is the substance of things hoped for, the evidence of things not seen. (Hebrews 11:1 KJV)

When I got demoted on my job, I couldn't see the new opportunity that would be created just for me three years later. "But if not" is how you walk out your faith. There is often a time gap between a promise from God and the realization of the promise.

"But if not" is how you live in between.
As we process life's hurts and disappointments we must proclaim "But if not."

Our God is able, and He will, but even if He does not change our situation, we will not bow down to the craziness of the world around us.

Prayer:

Oh Lord, our God, and our Redeemer. Thank you for being a God of not only our mountaintops but our valleys. Please help us remember You always have our best interests at heart. A no or closed door is never the end. We are so thankful You are in charge of results.

Amen

Dance Steps:

1. Write "But if not" on an index card and tape it to your bathroom mirror.
2. Be sure to look at the index card at least twice a day and read the words out loud.
3. Listen to the song "Even If" by MercyMe

The Stockdale Paradox-Honesty

"You must retain faith that you will prevail in the end, regardless of the difficulties.

AND at the same time… You must confront the most brutal facts of your current reality, whatever they might be."-Admiral Jim Stockdale

When it was evident my marriage was unraveling…I was enraged. Yes because of my ex-husband's last affair… but we dealt with serial infidelity, so honestly and sadly, it wasn't just that he cheated on me, AGAIN.

See, we had a deal:

While he worked several states away in a management trainee program, I would stay in North Carolina, work and take care of our girls. Once he landed the dream job that was promised after finishing the program, we were going to move and do life differently. I can still remember us dreaming of our new life: we were going to live minimally, save and eliminate debt AND I wouldn't work at first. I would FINALLY be able to take a well-deserved break from trying to "do-it-all" and be able to concentrate on just being a wife and mom.

When things got tough while my ex-husband was away, I encouraged myself by saying "this is just temporary."

When work became unbearable, I said; "this is temporary."

When I was tired after soccer, dance, piano and a sassy mouthed thirteen year old, I would say, "This is just temporary."

Then one day I realized, my ex-husband was NEVER going to rescue me.

I. WAS. DEVASTATED.

My ex-husband could not rescue me. It was not his job.

The truth was: I had put my ex-husband on the throne instead of God.

When I was encouraging myself saying "this is just temporary," I was right…it was just temporary, just like everything else on earth. But when I got truthful and accepted my piece of the pie I could admit…people treat you the way you allow them to treat you AND I was depending on the wrong source.

Then Jesus turned to the Jews who had claimed to believe in him. "If you stick with this, living out what I tell you, you are my disciples for sure. Then you will experience for yourselves the truth, and the truth will free you." (John 8:32 The Message)

Truth sets me free, but it is not always comfortable. It's when we live out what God instructs us to do that we experience the freedom of truth.

When I am not truthful with myself or refuse to accept the reality of what is, I end up doing stuff that doesn't work for me. Dishonesty can become a catalyst to relationships that are dysfunctional, jobs we actively dislike, and addictions to hide the things we don't want other people to see and we really don't want to deal with.

Once I got honest, truth allowed me to begin to patiently and joyfully endure and finally put my faith in who is in charge of circumstances, to begin with.

What is the truth about your situation?

Prayer:

Dear God,

Thank you for the opportunity to be honest. Dealing with the truth is sometimes difficult, but nothing is too hard for you. Please help us keep our eyes focused on what is true.

Amen

Dance Steps:

1. Write out the truth about your most recent or bothersome hurt (the whole truth—ugly parts and all.)

_____

_____

_____

_____

_____

_____

_____

2. Remember, it's when we live out what God instructs us to do that we experience the freedom of truth. What do you feel like God is calling you to do next?

_____

_____

_____

_____

_____

_____

_____

3. What if God does not change your situation?

_____

_____

_____

_____

_____

_____

Stockdale Paradox-Willingness

FOR THE PAST COUPLE OF days, we have been learning from Admiral Stockdale's story and wise words. When asked how he was able to endure being captured and tortured during the Vietnam War, Admiral Stockdale shared what Jim Collins called "The Stockdale Paradox" in his book *Good to Great.*

What is even more interesting than the paradox itself is Admiral Stockdale said "the optimists" were the first prisoners to die in the concentration camp:

"They were the ones who said, 'We're going to be out by Christmas.' And Christmas would come, and Christmas would go. Then they'd say, 'We're going to be out by Easter.' And Easter would come, and Easter would go. And then Thanksgiving, and then it would be Christmas again. And they died of a broken heart."

Instead of taking an ostrich approach of burying his head in the sand and merely hoping for a better day like the optimists, Admiral Stockdale created a tapping system for the prisoners to communicate while in solitary confinement. He also devised a timed milestone system to help prisoners cope with being tortured.

Admiral Stockdale combined faith with brutal honesty and a willingness to take action.

As I began to write this devotional, I was initially excited and energized to write about the things God shared with me. But when old feelings started to stir, and the reality of handling a blended family wreaked havoc on my schedule, my willingness could not be found. I wanted to write, but the process was painstaking and time-consuming.

Just like the optimists, I set unrealistic goals for myself and became disenfranchised when I could not meet my expectations. I asked myself questions like: "Why even write a book?" "Who is even going to read it?" But to finish the book, I had to be willing to write when it was not convenient and follow through by actually writing—even if no one ever read my words.

Our infamous Hebrew boys were willing to be put into the fiery furnace without 100 percent assurance God would rescue them. Their willingness became action when King Nebuchadnezzar ordered his soldiers to tie the boys up and throw them into the furnace. (Daniel 3:19)

Once the boys fell into the furnace, the king was astonished to see them walking around inside the fire. He went from astonished to confused as he realized the boys were not walking around in the fire by themselves. (We aren't either!!!)

> ...."But I see four men unbound, walking in the midst of the fire, and they are not hurt; and the appearance of the fourth is like a son of the gods." (Daniel 3:25)

Immediately, the King commanded the boys to come out of the fire, and they did. Everyone was amazed to see not even a hair on their heads was burned. They didn't even smell like fire. (Daniel 3:26-27)

> Nebuchadnezzar answered and said, "Blessed be the God of Shadrach, Meshach, and Abednego, who has sent his angel and delivered his servants, who trusted in him, and set aside the king's command, and yielded up their bodies rather than serve and worship any god except their own God. Therefore I make a decree: Any people, nation, or language that speaks anything against the God of Shadrach, Meshach, and Abednego shall be torn limb from limb, and their houses laid in ruins, for there is

no other god who is able to rescue in this way." Then the king promoted Shadrach, Meshach, and Abednego in the province of Babylon. Daniel 3:28-30 ESV

Because they had faith in God that they would prevail, and faced the reality He could choose not to help them, yet were still willing to do what was difficult…..they were protected and promoted.

In the book of Isaiah, there is a promise tied to willingness:

If you are willing and obedient, you shall eat the good of the land (Isaiah 1:19)ESV

If we want to "eat the good of the land" (move on with our lives healthy and whole), we must be honest about our situation, remain faithful, and be willing to take God-directed action without seeing signs of good results on the horizon.

Prayer:

Dear God,

Thank you for being the source of our protection and promotion. Please help us remain willing. Refresh our thinking with the assurance that as the furnaces of our lives threaten to burn us, You are right there with us in the midst of the fire.

Amen

Dance Steps:

1. Willingness involves opening our minds and being receptive to change. What changes in your life have you been unwilling to accept?

_____

_____

_____

_____

_____

_____

_____

_____

2. When we are willing, we recognize we do not have all the answers and become humble enough to learn from our experiences and other people. What have you learned from your most recent hurt?

_____

_____

_____

_____

_____

_____

_____

_____

Gratitude-Contentment

When I was part of the host team at my church, all of the volunteers met before the worship experience for a "volunteer rally." During the rally, Pastor Greg would often say inspirational things to get us pumped up and remind us of the importance of our jobs. One cold morning, he deviated from his usual statements and challenged each person to use gratitude to create and or change our atmosphere.

Pastor Greg said we should bring our atmosphere to a place instead of letting the place or the people in it dictate our attitude. Although he was talking about our attitudes as volunteers, his words became an "aha" moment for me.

As I attempted to move on with my life post-divorce, I accepted the way things were, but I wished they were different. I was annoyed by being a single mom, my job, my finances, and on and on. When Pastor Greg asked us to change our atmosphere with gratitude, I'm pretty sure I sucked my teeth.

I was at a place in my life I never dreamed I would be. What was gratitude going to do to change my situation?

In retrospect, I can hear God saying; "I'm so glad you asked. Being thankful and expressing gratitude despite your preferences develops contentment."

WOW.

The Apostle Paul said:

...I have learned in whatever situation I am to be content. I know how to be brought low, and I know how to abound. In any and every circumstance, I have learned the secret of facing plenty and hunger, abundance and need. I can do all things through him who strengthens me. (Philippians 4:11-13) ESV

When Pastor Greg challenged us to change our personal atmosphere with gratitude, I thanked God for His provision, my health, my children, my job, friends, and a church family. Surprisingly, my atmosphere and attitude changed at least for a little while.

Walking the path of healing has been a long process. Being thankful one morning at church was not enough. I had to make gratitude a daily habit.

Gratitude produces perspective and allows us to see our lives through the lens of contentment.

Contentment releases us from the need for things to be different.

Through Pastor Greg's challenge, God distracted me from focusing on what I was lacking to concentrating on living.

How can you focus on living today?

Prayer:

Dear God,

Thank you for being such an amazing Father. Lord forgive us for not expressing gratitude for all the things you do for us daily. We take so much for granted. Help us to exercise our gratitude muscle so we can be strong enough to focus on living and the things that are going right.

Amen

Dance Steps:

1. Write down three things you are thankful for.

    i. _____

    ii. _____

    iii. _____

2. Think of a person who has been there for you or someone who did something kind for you. Write that person a "gratitude letter" letting them know how appreciative you are for what they did and/or your relationship with them.

Physically write the letter and either mail it to them or hand deliver it to them (text or email are too impersonal).

Gratitude-Praise & Worship

WHEN I WAS IN MIDDLE school, I really wished I knew how to fight. Although I did not have a ton of it, girl drama would sometimes sneak in and bump into my preteen-bliss. On top of not knowing how to fight, my parents were teachers, so they were not the "if someone hits you, you hit them back" kind of parents. No, my parents said if someone hits you, "tell the teacher." (Eye roll)

As an adult, I have sometimes still wished I knew how to fight- I mean like mixed martial arts style. Ever since playing the video game, *Mortal Kombat* in college, I have daydreams of being a total warrior princess who is stunning and kind but has the best "finishing move" to defeat her opponents.

I thought my divorce becoming final would be my perpetual "finishing move." I quickly learned life is not a video game. There are no winners in a divorce. There are only survivors who hopefully learn something about becoming a better person in the future.

The war of breaking entanglements with people after being hurt, rebuilding a life after losing a job, or continuing to apply in the face of receiving rejection letters can be gruesome. Often in these situations, we are outnumbered and even our best "Mortal Kombat finishing move" will not help us. Also, calculating, manipulating, and figuring out our next move on our own is equally as worthless.

God urged me to use the secret weapons of praise and worship instead of brute force to help me forge ahead into my new life post-divorce.

Praise is an outward expression of approval or admiration and can be given to God and others. When given to God, praise distracts our minds away from our troubles, refocuses our minds onto Him and all He has done, and reminds us of His presence.

Worship goes a little deeper than praise. Worshipping God involves humility and surrender and is given based on who God is versus what He has done.

The Biblical account of King Jehoshaphat provides us with a "praise war strategy" manual.

…Some men came and told Jehoshaphat, "A great multitude is coming against you"…then Jehoshaphat was afraid and set his face to seek the LORD…(2 Chronicles 20:2-3)ESV

Jehoshaphat, just like us, was fearful about his next steps but he went to God for guidance.

After seeking guidance, God responded to Jehoshaphat:

…Thus says the Lord to you, "Do not be afraid and do not be dismayed at this great horde, for the battle is not yours but God's. 2 Chronicles 20:15 ESV

God told Jehoshaphat to keep his head up, go on do the hard thing and know that HE would be with him all the way.

After consulting the people, Jehoshaphat appointed men to sing to the LORD and to praise Him for the splendor of His holiness as they went out at the head of the army, saying: **"Give thanks to the LORD, for his love endures forever." 2 Chronicles 20:21 ESV**

Jehoshaphat thanked God because His love endures forever.

It is easy to praise God and tell others about Him when things are going well. Easy praise, although worthwhile, doesn't cost me anything. It is not a sacrifice.

It is when a spouse leaves, a child is defiant, there is more month than money, my heart is broken, the medical test is not favorable...it is in these times praise is the last thing I think about doing, but it is the most effective method of battle.

I finally began to offer my "sacrifice of praise," when I chose to believe even though life was not going as I thought it should, God was and is still good and could be trusted. When I felt unsettled, I turned on worship music or simply got on my knees in solemn reverence to my God.

When we get distracted with praise and worship there is a reward:

And the kingdom of Jehoshaphat was at peace, for his God had given him rest on every side. 2 Chronicles 20:30 ESV

The reward of praise and worship is peace.

Can you offer God a sacrifice of praise not because everything is perfect but because you trust HIM?

Prayer:

Dear God,

Thank you for being such an amazing Heavenly Father, who knows our needs before we can even get our bearings. We praise You for always being with us. Keep us ever mindful of the weapons of praise and worship because in them we find peace.

Amen

Dance Steps:

1. Listen to "Holy Spirit" by Francesca Battistelli while sitting on the floor or kneeling. While listening, place your hands on your knees with your palms facing the ceiling. Praise God for just being God.

2. In what ways can you make praise and worship part of your everyday life?

_____

_____

_____

_____

_____

_____

_____

_____

Gratitude-Serve

MY FRIENDS ARE GRACIOUS WOMEN who never seemed to mind me yapping their ears off with all my pre, during, and post-divorce stories. In fact, they often called me or sent sweet text messages to encourage me. The bulk of our conversations, coffee dates, and dinners were spent talking about my life and my feelings.

The love, care, and attention I received from my friends were vital for my healing process. However, with all of the focus being about me, it was easy to miss important things going on in their lives. Attention, positive or negative is addictive, and I had to break the cycle of "all eyes on me."

It became evident: being laser-focused on my issues did not bring true healing. God distracted me from being the star of my own show to being an "extra." Both of my children were involved in activities, so I made the very hard decision to decrease my ZUMBA® classes and serve them. I know that seems like a "well-that-is-what-moms-do" thing but teaching my ZUMBA® class was the one place I felt successful, and the ladies in my class give off amazing energy.

At my previous job, I took on the role of encourager despite feeling salty because I was passed over for a promotion. Trust me, it was all God. When I left, I still had not been promoted, but the heartfelt words my co-workers wrote in my cards were things that should have been written to a CEO.

As the years went by, people began to ask me to reach out to friends who were also going through break-ups. I had the awesome opportunity to pray with and for several women and their relationships. The conversations were not all about divorce. Some marriages/relationships were reconciled, which was glorious to witness. Others were not, but seeing broken women begin to smile again was priceless.

When God distracted me from being the "star" to an "extra," He was actually calling me to serve others.

Jesus is our ultimate example of a servant.

Just before being crucified, Jesus washed the disciples' feet at the last supper. This was a big deal because people during Biblical times did not have enclosed shoes like we have today. If they had shoes at all, they were probably sandals, and their roads were not paved. So with all the things their feet came in contact with, it is easy to imagine the disciples' feet were probably disgusting.

Peter tried to stop Jesus from washing his feet, but Jesus did not listen:

> **When he had finished washing their feet, he put on his clothes and returned to his place. "Do you understand what I have done for you?" he asked them. "You call me 'Teacher' and 'Lord,' and rightly so, for that is what I am. Now that I, your Lord and Teacher, have washed your feet, you also should wash one another's feet. I have set you an example that you should do as I have done for you. Very truly I tell you, no servant is greater than his master, nor is a messenger greater than the one who sent him. Now that you know these things, you will be blessed if you do them." (John 13:12-17 ESV)**

Jesus washing the disciples' feet and then challenging them to do the same for each other is a calling for us. We are being called to serve other people even if it means performing mundane tasks, and ignoring our pride, position, and comfort.

When we serve others and expect nothing in return, Jesus tells us we will be blessed. (John 12:17)

The blessing Jesus promised has been proven scientifically. A study published in the *International Journal of Psychophysiology* found people who give social support had lower blood pressure, reported receiving more social support, had higher self-esteem, less depression, and less stress than participants who did not give social support to others.

Serving others is a win-win.

As life ebbs and flows, we have a choice. Will we be consumed with our circumstances, schedule, and wants or will we become distracted with serving others?

Prayer:

Dear God,

Thank you for the opportunity to serve. We repent of making everything about us. Please help us recognize people in need and give us the motivation to provide a helping hand.

Amen

Dance Steps:

1. Ask God to show you opportunities to serve.
2. Serve in your own family! (What can you do with an attitude of joy—cook, clean, wash a car, cut the grass or help in your home or in the home of a family member?)

The High Road-Take It

No MATTER HOW YOU FEEL about First Lady Michelle Obama, her famous slogan: "When they go low, we go high" is excellent advice.

When my ex-husband moved back into town without discussion and asking for significant changes in our custody and child support agreements, a mere two weeks before my wedding to my current husband, I gritted my teeth and took the high road. I asked my girls what they wanted to do and I yielded to their wishes, despite my pride. I never wanted them to tell the story of how their mom kept them from their father. People told me I should go back to court. However, life has taught me to go to God in prayer first. God told me three words: LET IT GO.

Really God?

I would be lying if I said in agreeing to my ex-husband's terms I didn't feel like I was the one always losing. I would also be lying if I said agreeing was easy. When I looked back at why I sought a divorce in the first place, my end game - what I was truly searching for - was peace. It wasn't having the top place, getting the most money, winning (there are no winners in divorce), or making my ex suffer.

When someone has hurt us, we have a choice about which road we will take. We can go low and do and say whatever feels good at the moment. Or, we can go high by walking away and saying nothing or by exercising our boundaries and expressing our feelings without malice and negativity.

The story of Abraham and Lot gives us a Biblical example of the high road and the low road.

And Lot, who went with Abram, also had flocks and herds and tents, so that the land could not support both of them dwelling together; for their possessions were so great that they could not dwell together, and there was strife between the herdsmen of Abram's livestock and the herdsmen of Lot's livestock. At that time the Canaanites and the Perizzites were dwelling in the land.

Then Abram said to Lot, "Let there be no strife between you and me, and between your herdsmen and my herdsmen, for we are kinsmen. Is not the whole land before you? Separate yourself from me. If you take the left hand, then I will go to the right, or if you take the right hand, then I will go to the left." (Genesis 13:5-8 ESV)

Abram, (whose name had not been changed to Abraham yet), was Lot's uncle and he actually owned the property. If you follow the rules of business, the person who owns or has the most usually gets to pick first. Abram took the high road by allowing Lot to choose which land he wanted first.

And Lot lifted up his eyes and saw that the Jordan Valley was well watered everywhere like the garden of the Lord, like the land of Egypt, in the direction of Zoar. (This was before the Lord destroyed Sodom and Gomorrah.) So Lot chose for himself all the Jordan Valley, and Lot journeyed east. Thus they separated from each other. Abram settled in the land of Canaan, while Lot settled among the cities of the valley and moved his tent as far as Sodom. Now the men of Sodom were wicked, great sinners against the Lord. (Genesis 13:10-13 ESV)

Lot took advantage of his uncle's kindness. Lot saw what looked comfortable and took the low road right on down to Sodom without asking God where he should go. But as is always the case with "low road behavior," consequences lurk in the crevices waiting for an inopportune time to seep out. Then what seemed so appealing loses its luster, and there is no peace.

The high road is all about peace. I am so thankful for peace.

Abram was willing to take "a loss" to gain peace. Abram's "loss" was more than regained in the promise God gave him after he allowed Lot to choose first.

The Lord said to Abram after Lot had parted from him, "Look around from where you are, to the north and south, to the east and west. All the land that you see I will give to you and your offspring forever. I will make your offspring like the dust of the earth, so that if anyone could count the dust, then your offspring could be counted. Go, walk through the length and breadth of the land, for I am giving it to you." (Genesis 13: 14-17 ESV)

I love the way Matthew Henry's Commentary sums things up: "God will abundantly make up in spiritual peace, what we lose for preserving neighborly peace."

Prayer:

Dear God,

Thank you for being a gracious God who always has an eye on our lives. We praise you for the opportunity to extend grace and take the high road because of the grace, comfort, and love you have given us. Please help us to remember your great works so that our focus can be sharpened by perspective.

Amen

Dance Steps:

1. Write about a time you went down the low road:

_____

_____

_____

_____

_____

_____

_____

_____

2. How did you feel after going down the low road?

_____

_____

_____

_____

_____

_____

_____

3. What are some ways you can take the high road but not be a doormat?

_____

_____

_____

_____

_____

_____

_____

High Road-Don't Seek Revenge

ONE ORDINARY WEDNESDAY, I CHECKED my personal email at work just before leaving for the day. I had an email from a very dear lady in my ZUMBA® class. I opened the email expecting to find a question about the class or a reminder to get a receipt book. What I saw instead left me stunned, hurt, hot-faced, and as if the wind had been knocked out of my sails.

The email asked me to step up my instructing in class, bring new routines and/or learn ones from other instructors, and make the workout more intense. It contained language like "several of us feel like" and "we discussed."

As lovely as new routines, better music, emulating other instructors and making the workout more intense sounded, I did not have anything else to give. Perhaps my plastic "everything-is-ok" smile kept them from knowing it took every ounce of energy I had to keep working, single mommying and teaching in the face of my life as I knew it was melting in the fire of divorce.

I felt like I had been punched in the stomach by their collective suggestions and I was angry at their timing. The author and those quoted in the email knew what I was going through. With some hindsight perspective, I can see the email as constructive criticism, just with horrible timing.

However, when the email was fresh, I pretended to take their criticism graciously and was not honest about my feelings being hurt. I stayed up late drilling out new routines and ramped up the music only to get a half nod or more criticism from them on my choreography. When they did not applaud my attempts to do what they asked, I became bitter.

I sought revenge through distancing myself. What was once a tight-knit friendship built around a shared love of dance, felt yucky. I hated their expectations and those of what seemed like everyone else for me to "just get over it already" and return to life as usual. Whatever life as usual meant.

I played the words of the email over in my mind continuously. Luckily, I did not make a general announcement to everyone, but I wish I had been in a healthier place when the email came. My "revenge" of the silent treatment did not help me feel better. I actually felt worse, and I wanted to quit teaching and life in general.

Revenge is like that. It makes you think getting even, paying them back, or hurting them will avenge you. But, it does not, and you often regret your behavior later.

God is so wise, and He knows what is best for us. Perhaps that is why Paul provided us with a map of how to behave when we have been wronged.

Repay no one evil for evil, but give thought to do what is honorable in the sight of all. If possible, so far as it depends on you, live peaceably with all. Beloved, never avenge yourselves, but leave it to the wrath of God, for it is written, "Vengeance is mine, I will repay, says the Lord." Romans 12: 16-19 ESV

I love the words: "as far as it depends on you live peaceably with all." Those are direct words to my heart. My behavior is where my control lies. When I seek revenge, I am attempting to control results. Results are God's department.

Eventually, my heart was softened, and God distracted me from focusing on what they said and how I felt onto how I could continue to bless women in my class. I felt God say to me, "Keep showing up." So I did.

Several regulars left my class for other ZUMBA® instructors or other fitness formats and at first, it seemed like words in the email were true. But, I kept showing up, and I stopped putting pressure on myself to create new routines or be any other instructor other than me.

Over time, new ladies came to class, and they had no idea the old routines were old. One night after class, a woman ran up to me at the end beaming. She hugged me tight and said she was excited we did some of the old routines because she had surgery with a very long and challenging recovery. "I was afraid I would be lost and wouldn't know any of the routines but being back feels like coming home," she said.

God distracted me from focusing on what they said, how I felt, and how to hurt them in return by shifting my focus to continuing to show up. Continuing to show up allowed me to be thankful for the ladies who remained in class and the new ones who came instead of concentrating on the few who were discontented and left.

Continuing to show up to our lives by being thankful for what is there in the moment instead of focusing on what was taken, what someone did, or how to pay them back is how we take the high road towards peace.

Prayer:

Dear God,

Thank you for your grace, mercy, and love. Forgive us for the many times we manipulated and plotted ways to hurt others in response to being hurt. We trust you, and we know the circumstances of our lives may take us by surprise, but you are never surprised and are always ready.

Amen

Dance Steps:

1. Write about a time you sought revenge.

_____
_____
_____
_____
_____
_____
_____
_____

2. How did you feel after you "paid them back" or "gave them a piece of your mind"?

_____
_____
_____
_____
_____
_____
_____
_____

3. What steps can you take to refocus your perspective to "showing up and noticing what is going right"?

_____
_____
_____
_____
_____
_____
_____
_____

High Road-Pray for Your Offender

I HAD THE GREAT PLEASURE of going back to my alma mater for home-coming and to celebrate my twenty-fifth anniversary of being inducted into my sorority. One of the highlights from my trip was taking a legacy photo at the Old Well in the middle of the campus with the majority of the phenomenal women I became a Delta with so many years ago. On our way to take the picture, one of my sorority sisters and I took selfies, cracked jokes, and ended up giggling and belly laughing just like when we were college girls.

My sorority sister sighed and said, "I really miss you, and I wish we could hang out, but _____ isn't ready." She was referring to her husband. When I was married the first time, my sorority sister and her husband were one of our "couple friends." Her husband and my ex-husband became very close friends, and they often did guy things without us, and they are still good friends.

She went on to say her husband was "heartbroken" about my ex and me no longer being together and was unwilling to be around me because I had remarried.

Her words were like daggers into my heart. How could he be upset with me for remarrying yet not be upset with my ex for having extra-marital affairs? I didn't expect him to no longer be a friend to my ex but why was I now the enemy? As we continued to walk, my pulse quickened, and I batted away angry tears. He was heartbroken? Oh really?

The next few moments were a blur. I remember telling my sorority sister her husband's inability to be around me because I sought a divorce and remarried two years AFTERWARDS was like co-signing on my ex's behavior. She disagreed. I politely walked away from her pretending to be preoccupied with where to stand for our group picture.

I stewed for several more minutes. I was angry and sad. Nobody tells you this part of a divorce. The part where people choose sides and their choosing hurts down deep because you thought your relationship with them was different.

I made the best of the rest of the day but was shaken on the inside. My emotions went from well, if they don't want to be around me…it's their loss to being tearful like a little girl who wasn't chosen to be on the kickball team.

Later that evening, my sorority sister sent me a text asking me to send her copies of some of the photos we took earlier that day. Every fiber of my body wanted to ignore her or strike up the conversation again about how wrong she and her husband were. Send her pictures? PLUH-EASE! (Insert eye and neck roll here!)

I furiously began to type a "piece of my mind" to her when I felt God tugging on my heart and distracting me away from how I felt. I deleted my text and began to pray. I prayed about how I felt and then as if like a teenager who mutters "fiiiiiinnnnne" as they begin to do what they are told, I gritted my teeth and prayed for my sorority sister and her husband. I also prayed for my ex because the entire situation brought up my hurt feelings from the affairs and divorce all over again. I know it sounds "churchy," but I felt an inner nudging to go to God about it all. What was the alternative? Be resentful and bitter while my sorority sister and her husband went about their lives totally unbothered because it wasn't their situation anyway? No thanks.

Jesus gave specific instructions on how we are to treat people who hurt us.

But I say to you, Love your enemies and pray for those who persecute you, so that you may be sons of your Father who is in heaven. For he makes his sun rise on the evil and on the good, and sends rain on the just and on the unjust. Matthew 5:44-45 ESV

Although praying for those who hurt us is not the first thing that comes to mind in the aftermath of being offended, it actually moves us down the path towards healing much faster.

When I prayed for my sorority sister and her husband, it was a quick basic prayer for both of them and their marriage. That was all I could do and be genuine. I honestly hoped they would never have to experience the gut-wrenching heartache of divorce and the fall out of family and friends that occurs as a result.

After I prayed, my attitude was a little better. I pulled up the silly self-ies my sorority sister and I had taken just a few hours before and smiled. I sent the photos to her without a word about our previous conversation.

My sorority sister and I had the opportunity to have coffee about a month after homecoming. I was able to bring up my feelings without anger and she clarified her husband was not upset with me but was having a hard time adjusting to my divorce. (Sigh) All in all, I enjoyed our coffee date. How our relationship ebbs and flows in the future is up to God, and I feel peaceful about it.

Although I am peaceful, I am also a recovering people pleaser. I would be lying if I said my sorority sister's husband being upset about my divorce doesn't still bother me when something happens that jars my memory about it. God is teaching me to use those reminders as opportunities to pray for them. Not only does praying for them change my attitude it also refocuses my energy on what I can control…my behavior.

To say that "prayer changes things" is not as close to the truth as saying, "Prayer changes me, and then I change things." God has established things so that prayer, on the basis of redemption, changes the way a person looks at things. Prayer is not a matter of changing things externally, but one of working miracles in a person's inner nature. -- Oswald Chambers

Prayer:

Dear God,

Thank you for Jesus and His life that serves as a roadmap for us as we navigate our lives. Sharpen our senses to hear and feel you nudging us to pray for those who hurt us. Give us the courage to pray and offer grace instead of retaliating.

Amen

Dance Step:
Write out a prayer for someone who hurt you.

_____

_____

_____

_____

_____

_____

_____

_____

_____

_____

_____

_____

_____

_____

_____

_____

_____

_____

_____

_____

_____

_____

WHEN SOMEONE HURTS US, WE
HAVE A CHOICE OF WHICH ROAD
WE WILL TAKE.

WE CAN GO LOW AND DO OR SAY
WHATEVER FEELS GOOD AT THE
MOMENT.

OR, WE CAN GO
HIGH BY
WALKING AWAY
OR EXPRESSING
OUR FEELINGS
WITHOUT MALICE
AND NEGATIVITY.

Forgiveness-The Next Step

OFTEN THE GOD-DIRECTED ACTION AFTER being hurt is forgiveness. A quick Google search will bring up varying definitions of forgiveness with a common theme. God impressed upon my heart: forgiveness means giving up resentment or a claim to get even.

A small child named Ruby Bridges embodied forgiveness and carried the weight of our country's civil rights movement around her six-year-old neck. In November of 1960, Ruby Bridges became the first African American student to integrate an elementary school in the South. Ruby and her family faced horrific persecution, and she attended school all year in a class as the only student with her teacher, Barbara Henry.

Ruby's daily walk into William Franz Elementary School resembled a war zone more than a schoolyard. Angry adults yelled racial slurs at her daily as she was escorted into the school building by US Federal Marshals.

Ruby's teacher became especially fond of her saying Ruby never missed a day of school and despite all that was going on around her, remained a pleasant student. One school morning, Ruby's teacher watched as Ruby stopped in front of the screaming mob and appeared to be talking. Worried she may suffer some type of psychological trauma from the current events in her life, Ruby was offered counseling by Dr. Robert Coles.

Dr. Coles asked Ruby what she said to the crowd. Ruby's response was astounding: "I wasn't talking, I was praying for them." Dr. Coles asked her why she prayed, and Ruby answered, "Well, don't you think they need praying for?" Completely intrigued, Dr. Coles then asked what she prayed. Ruby responded: "Please, Dear God, forgive them because they don't know what they're doing."

At the tender age of six, Ruby chose to forgive instead of resenting and lashing out at those who hated her for something she could not change...her skin color. Ruby's prayer was a direct "prayer quote" from Jesus when He was on the cross suffering for sins He did not commit.

And Jesus said, "Father, forgive them, for they know not what they do." (Luke 23:34 ESV)

Although tortured, Jesus forgave. He forgave those who hurt Him, and He forgives us. Because of who He is and how He took the punishment for our sins, He gives us the strength to extend forgiveness to others. The cross was all about forgiveness.

It is a difficult concept to embrace when someone hurts us deliberately. God has helped me to see: although their actions may be purposeful, they cannot know the magnitude of the consequences caused by their actions until they occur.

Thinking of things this way has blessed me when processing through forgiving my ex-husband. I am 100% sure he knew his affairs were hurtful. However, I am also sure he did not know the extent of the pain, grief, heartbreak, and devastation that ensued.

Forgiving my ex-husband does not mean what he did was ok. Forgiving him does not mean I never think about our broken family or that my wounds are completely healed.

Forgiving him does not mean I "feel" like being forgiving.

Forgiving him means I actively choose not to hold what he did over him. It is NOT easy. There are good days of forgiveness and not-so-good days. There are starts, stops, mountaintops and long dark valleys on my path of forgiveness.

I am on a journey to become the woman God is calling me to be. My journey is uphill and requires light travel. The weight of seeking revenge, holding a grudge, or being bitter are too heavy to carry and cannot go with me where God is taking me.

You were taught, with regard to your former way of life, to put off your old self, which is being corrupted by its deceitful desires; to be made new in the attitude of your minds; and to put on the new self, created to be like God in true righteousness and holiness. Ephesians 4:22-24 NIV

God is calling all of us to grow and change.
Unforgiveness keeps us tied to the old versions of ourselves.

Prayer:

Dear God,
   Thank you for Jesus. Thank you for sacrificing your Son so we can access grace and extend grace to others. Forgiveness is difficult, but nothing is too hard for You. As we continue down our paths of becoming who You have called us to be, we express gratitude for who You are in our lives.
   Amen

Dance Steps:

1. Think of a situation you are holding or held a grudge about. How does/did holding the grudge make you feel? (Write about your feelings.)

_____

_____

_____

_____

_____

_____

_____

_____

2. What are your thoughts on viewing forgiveness as giving up resentment or a claim to get even? (Write about your feelings)

_____

_____

_____

_____

_____

_____

_____

_____

_____

_____

_____

_____

_____

_____

_____

_____

_____

_____

_____

_____

_____

Forgiveness is a Command

MY PARENTS WERE BOTH "OLD school" teachers, so there were a lot of rules in our home. Education was a major priority, so there was no "my head hurts" and you got to stay out of school or any excuse taken for not completing assignments. There was also no excuse accepted for breaking curfew (because you should have left wherever you were earlier to account for traffic), and "because I said so" was a cover all statement that had no rebuttal!

Forgiveness falls in the "because I said so" category. It is one of the things we are commanded to do, and it reminds us we have been forgiven and did not get what we surely deserved.

When teaching the disciples how to pray, Jesus had a lot to say about forgiveness.

"Give us this day our daily bread. And forgive us our debts, as we have forgiven our debtors" [letting go of both the wrong and the resentment]. Matthew 6:11-12 AMP

For if you forgive others their trespasses [their reckless and willful sins], your heavenly Father will also forgive you. But if you do not forgive others [nurturing your hurt and anger with the result that it interferes with your relationship with God], then your Father will not forgive your trespasses. Matthew 6:14-15 (AMP)

Jesus' words spark a wrestling match between how we feel and what we know we have been commanded to do. I love how the Amplified version silences us when it defines forgiveness as "letting go of both the wrong and the resentment", trespasses as "their reckless and willful sins" and unforgiveness as "nurturing your hurt and anger."

Here are some truths God revealed to me about forgiveness:

Forgiveness is required and involves giving up resentment or a claim to get even.

Forgiveness is not saying, "I forgive you" or accepting an apology.

Forgiveness requires a spiritual and emotional change on the inside of the person who has been hurt.

Annnnnnd...forgiveness is not painless! Sometimes just thinking about forgiveness gets us "all in our feelings" and we begin to ask some tough questions:

When we forgive someone, does that mean what he or she did is excused?

Forgiveness does not excuse their behavior. Forgiveness chooses to no longer hold what they did over them.

What about consequences... don't they have to pay for what they did?

Forgiveness does not erase responsibility. It includes accountability and grace.

Beloved, never avenge yourselves, but leave the way open for God's wrath [and His judicial righteousness]. Romans 12:19 AMP

I stunted my own healing by being so focused on consequences for my ex-husband. God distracted me from worrying about what did or did not happen to him by allowing me to see forgiveness as a way to accept my reality and begin to move on with my life.

Does forgiveness mean we have to reconcile the relationship?

Reconciliation is a noble possibility and should be prayerfully pursued (especially in marriage), but it is not required. The decision to reconcile a relationship is personal and requires a great deal of prayer and wise counsel.

Forgiveness and reconciliation although often thought of together, are not the same. You can forgive someone and not continue in a relationship with them.

Forgiveness is a duet between God and me. Reconciliation is a group performance between God, them, and me.

Forgiveness has no strings attached to it. Reconciliation has fringe!

Reconciliation requires conviction, repentance, honest and specific confession of harm, a process of rebuilding trust by the offender and willingness by the person offended. Rebuilding trust hinges on trustworthy behavior.

The Prodigal Son demanded his inheritance before his father died. He took his inheritance, went to another country, squandered his money and suffered through a famine. "When he came to his senses" (Luke 15:17), he decided to go back home.

"But while he was still a long way off, his father saw him and was filled with compassion for him; he ran to his son, threw his arms around him and kissed him. "The son said to him, 'Father, I have sinned against heaven and against you. I am no longer worthy to be called your son.' "But the father said to his servants, 'Quick! Bring the best robe and put it on him. Put a ring on his finger and sandals on his feet. Bring the fattened calf and kill it. Let's have a feast and celebrate. For this son of mine was dead and is alive again; he was lost and is found" Luke 15:21-24 ESV

The father had already forgiven his son because when he saw him from far away, he ran out to him. Their relationship was reconciled by the father's willingness and the son's conviction and repentance.

We are commanded to forgive those who hurt us because we have been forgiven.

If God is leading you towards reconciliation and restoration in your spirit be patient, pray fervently, contend for the relationship, and be willing.

Prayer:

Dear God,

Thank you for the gift of forgiveness. We are a forgiven people who have done wrong on so many occasions. Yet, your mercies are new for us every morning. Help us to have the strength to fight through how we feel and forgive those who hurt us. We know forgiving those who harm us is not excusing their behavior. Forgiveness is giving up our right to be resentful and pay them back. Please keep our hearts softened towards reconciliation and restoration of our relationships.

Amen.

Dance Steps:

1. Write a forgiveness letter to someone who hurt you recently or in the past (the person does not have to be alive). It is okay to express your disappointment or hurt but finish the letter by stating you will no longer hold what they did over them.)

2. How can you remind yourself to practice forgiveness?

_____

_____

_____

_____

_____

_____

_____

_____

_____

Forgiveness is a Process

"DESPITE HUNDREDS OF SERMONS ON forgiveness, we do not forgive easily, nor find ourselves easily forgiven. Forgiveness, we discover, is always harder than the sermons make it out to be." –Elizabeth O'Connor

Forgiveness may be a lot of really good things, but people who promote it seem to leave out a few critical details about forgiveness: forgiveness is easier said than done and it is often a long process. When someone cuts us down deep, the path of forgiveness is a long road full of ups, downs, setbacks and start again.

Lysa Terkeurst defined imperfect progress as "slow steps of change wrapped in grace." Forgiveness at it's best is imperfect progress.

Although the televised version or the "shared story" of forgiveness is a one-time event, forgiving a painful and gut-wrenching hurt is not a "one and done."

I was totally unprepared for the number of triggers I have experienced while healing from divorce: songs on the radio, conversations, social media posts, making financial decisions, and I could go on and on. Each time I am triggered, I feel hurt all over again. The degree of which I feel hurt sometimes depends on the trigger and sometimes does not make any sense at all.

Then Peter came and said to Him, "Lord, how often shall my brother sin against me and I forgive him? Up to seven times?"

Jesus said to him, "I do not say to you, up to seven times, but up to seventy times seven". Matthew 18:21-22 NIV

Just in case you missed Jesus' math, seventy times seven is four hundred and ninety!

God distracted me away from my hurt into dancing towards a choice. Every time I feel hurt from current or past offenses, I have a decision to make. Every time you feel hurt you have a decision to make too. We get to choose: will we be bitter or better.

The daily choice of better over bitter is the process of forgiveness.

The dictionary defines a process as a series of actions or steps taken to achieve a particular end. One frustrating thing about forgiveness is we know we are commanded to do it but how? God shared three specific steps for me to take to walk in forgiveness. More days than not, I have to take these forgiveness steps over and over.

Steps of Forgiveness:

Step 1
Acknowledge the hurt and pain.

As a "good Christian girl," I felt pressured to exude happiness and joy despite my true feelings. I was heartbroken, disappointed, discouraged, and frustrated. Yet I smiled and appeared to be a pillar of strength and inner fortitude. Pretending did not move me towards healing or forgiveness. God allowed me to see my feelings were important to Him. I am important to Him, and so are you.

Although wallowing in hurt feelings for an extended period of time is not healthy, not being honest with how you feel can be detrimental. Acknowledging my true feelings versus just ruminating over what was done meant I had to actually feel heartbroken, disappointed, discouraged, and frustrated. One of the reasons we hold on to what they did is because we don't want to feel the pain of what was done "full force."

The only logical thing to do with my raw emotions was to take them to my Heavenly Father, and He comforted me. My situation did not change immediately, but comfort came in various forms: prepared meals from friends, a kind word from a stranger, a heartfelt Mother's Day card from my daughters, a picture-perfect sunrise.

"Blessed are those who mourn, for they shall be comforted."
Matthew 5:4 (ESV)

Step 2
"Take the L".

"Taking the L" means taking the loss. A huge step down the path of forgiveness is making peace with what happened.

We make peace with what happened by accepting the loss of how we prayed and hoped things would be.

"Taking the L" is the very thing we do not want to do. Yet, saying "it is what it is" while knowing God is in control and will right any wrongs the way He sees fit, is critical to the gift of true forgiveness.

When we "take the L" we relinquish the right to get even.

When we "take the L" we surrender our will to keep defending ourselves or arguing our point.

When we "take the L" we stop manipulating people or situations towards the outcomes we are attached to.

When we "take the L" we stop viewing our offender as a monster and begin to see them as a fellow fallen human.

"Taking the L" is all about stuff we need to do independent of our offender.

"Taking the L" has nothing to do with their consequences legal or otherwise. Our culture keeps us focused on them and what they did. But, it is not about them.

"Taking the L" is about me. "Taking the L" is about you.

"Taking the L" is accepting what happened and all its pain but reframing the events through the lens of hope and trust in God.

"Taking the L" is how we finish our lives well. Our hurts are not our lives in total. When we accept what happened, learn from it, and make necessary personal changes versus being embittered by our offenses, we finish well.

> **… let us also lay aside every weight, and sin which clings so closely, and let us run with endurance the race that is set before us, looking to Jesus, the founder and perfecter of our faith... Hebrews 12:1b-2a ESV**

Step 3
Repeat steps one and two as necessary!

Remember Jesus' math….forgive 490 times? What He was really suggesting was always forgive….like to infinity. Yes over and over. He knew we would be triggered. He knew it would be demanding, but because of who He is we have a place to go when we are weak.

> **For we do not have a high priest who is unable to sympathize with our weaknesses, but one who in every respect has been tempted as we are, yet without sin. Let us then with confidence draw near to the throne of grace, that we may receive mercy and find grace to help in time of need. Hebrews 4:15-16 ESV**

Acknowledge your hurt, "take the L," and repeat.

Prayer:

> Precious Heavenly Father we thank you. We thank you for being so patient with us as we navigate our offenses. We praise you for always being with us and for providing us with the ultimate example of how to be in relationship with others…Jesus.
> Amen

Dance Step:

1. Write down one thing in your life that did not go as you wanted and you still struggle with the way things played out?

_____

_____

_____

_____

_____

_____

_____

_____

2. Were there any people who offended you in the situation? If so, write his or her name.

_____

_____

_____

_____

_____

_____

_____

3. How did what they did make you feel?

_____

_____

_____

_____

_____

_____

_____

4. How does it make you feel to know Jesus cares about your feelings?

_____

_____

_____

_____

_____

_____

_____

_____

_____

5. How can you take your feelings to Jesus? (Prayer, walk in nature, journaling...etc.)

_____

_____

_____

_____

_____

_____

_____

_____

6. What does "taking the L" look like for you?

_____

_____

_____

_____

_____

_____

_____

_____

Move On-Second String Quarterback

MY MIND HAS WON THE Indy 500 in ruminating about my divorce. In a strange and twisted way, the infidelity stories and the drama of the fall-out afterward became companions for me. I wanted things to be different. But they were not different, so I told the stories over and over, and I was good at telling those stories.

Have you ever retold painful stories?

Over time, I found myself feeling the urge to skip to the end in the middle of orating my own saga. God was saying...move on. When I felt God calling me to move on, I almost rolled my eyes. I knew moving on was a good idea. I knew dwelling in the past wasn't healthy but "move on"? Really God?

I did not want to move on, I wanted a do-over.

I wanted my old life.

I wanted to rewrite the past.

The LORD said to Samuel, "How long will you grieve over Saul since I have rejected him from being king over Israel? Fill your horn with oil, and go. I will send you to Jesse the Bethlehemite, for I have provided for myself a king among his sons." 1 Samuel 16:1 ESV

Saul was disobedient to the Lord, and the Lord revealed to Samuel that He was rejecting Saul. This greatly troubled Samuel. Samuel was Saul's mentor, and he had invested a great deal into Saul.

Have you ever invested so much in a person, a job, an idea that pride crept in and said, "not after all I have sacrificed?" So you dug your heels in and tried harder?

Sometimes trying harder is what we are supposed to do. But sometimes we need to move on.

God helped me realize I could not change what happened (as much as I wanted to), but I could change my reaction to what happened. God's command to Samuel: "Fill your horn with oil, and go..." was how I changed my reaction to what happened.

"Fill your horn with oil and go" for me meant—.STOP and START
STOP being pitiful and being a victim.
STOP looking sad.
STOP telling anyone who would listen how devastated I was.
STOP being worried about my ex-husband's new life.
START thinking about my own life.
START taking responsibility for my own happiness.

When God told Samuel to fill his horn with oil and go, He answered the "why" question my teenagers always seem to ask when I tell them to do something. God said, "Fill your horn with oil and go. I will send you to Jesse the Bethlehemite, for I have provided for myself a king among his sons."

Just as Samuel had anointed Saul with oil many years before, he would soon anoint David to succeed Saul. Although Samuel could not see it, God had a plan. God's plan required Samuel to move on with his life. Samuel had to make a choice to take action.

I had no idea, but God had a new king in mind for me. A man who pursued me like never before and was so kind and patient. Although divorce, remarriage, and a blended family was not the story I imagined, it is my story, and I am thankful. I am Mrs. Jeffrey Boyd.

I know God has a sense of humor because my husband LOVES sports and television…two things that are NOT my favorites. I think I have watched more football and basketball games in the last year than I have in my entire life. Although the games don't always hold my attention, I love being with my husband, and the stories of the players are always intriguing to me.

The University of Alabama's second string quarterback Jalen Hurts got to play in the fourth quarter of the 2018 SEC championship game when Tua Tagovailoa (the first string quarterback) left the game with an ankle injury. Jalen scored fourteen unanswered points in the fourth quarter and led his team to victory and the title of the number one seed. Although it sounds like a magical Disney movie ending, you have to know the backstory.

In 2016 and until the 2017 National Championship game, Jalen Hurts had been the first string quarterback. He was benched at halftime of the 2017 Championship game when his team was losing 13-0 and his coach put in the second-string freshman quarterback, Tua. Tua had a surprising performance and led the Alabama team to a fantastic comeback victory.

Over the spring and summer, Jalen and Tua competed against each other for the spot of the first-string quarterback. Tua won, so Jalen had to sit and watch. Jalen watched Tua have a great 2018 season and become a finalist for the coveted Heisman Trophy. I'm no sports strategist, but I am sure this was not how Jalen wanted things to turn out.

Rumors began to fly about Jalen leaving Alabama, but he continued to play second and worked with their new quarterback coach to improve his game. On December 1st, 2018, with Tua limping off the field, Jalen was put back in the game and went on to win for his team. When he kept the ball and ran it in for a touchdown, Tua was on the sidelines cheering for him.

I think what CBS tweeted about Jalen said it best:

"Jalen Hurts could've left Alabama after being benched.
He could've sulked.

He didn't.

He stayed ready.

He delivered when his team needed him.

He's achieved the ultimate redemption."

When the women of Galilee went to the tomb where Jesus was buried after being crucified, they did not find his body. Instead, two angels were in the tomb, and they asked the women and I believe us as well, a question:

…"Why do you look for the living among the dead? He is not here; he has risen! Luke 24:5b-6 ESV

What happened in the past and its old hurts are dead places.

Looking for happiness and purpose in achievement, outcomes, relationships, entertainment or anything other than Jesus is a dead place.

Jalen Hurts could have stayed focused on all he lost. He could have watched reruns of his old games when he was the number one quarterback ad nauseam. But he didn't. He held his head high and concentrated on getting ready for when God would put him back in the game.

I'm thankful God put me back in the game.

When Jeff and I decided to get married, God told me our marriage would be a story of redemption and would have the power to change generations. The story of divorce and brokenness would be rewritten for our children and our children's children.

How powerful!

Is it easy? Absolutely not and I would be lying if I said I don't have to fight the urge to look back at my old life. But just like Jalen, I can't be bothered with playing happy (inaccurate) reruns of old times. I've got to be ready because I'm in the game.

You are in your game.

We get ready and remain ready for the game of our lives by proclaiming Jesus is risen and letting the joy of God's redemption be our strength.

Prayer:

Dear God,

Praise You that Jesus is risen! He finished His task and brought redemption for the world. There is nothing we can do to deserve the gift of forgiveness Jesus provides. Allow us to bask in the joy of Jesus not being in the tomb when life attempts to bury our faith.

Amen

Dance Steps:

1. Write about some of the dead places in your life.

_____
_____
_____
_____
_____
_____
_____
_____

2. How can you move on from these dead spaces by preparing for when God puts you back in the game?

_____
_____
_____
_____
_____
_____
_____
_____
_____

Move On-With Obedience

THERE IS SOMETHING ABOUT BEING in the aftermath of heartbreak, loss, rejection or betrayal that places us in a "middle zone" of longingly looking back or wishing for a better future. The "middle zone" is where we say "why me" and then daydream by saying "if I had ____then I would be happy."

The world around us tells us pursuing happiness is the way to move on with our lives. Although it sounds good, getting whatever we think we need to be happy is an illusion. When we get the new car, the new job, the new boo, there are new problems that go along with all of those things and then there are new achievements to get. So we scurry off to achieve more and put our happiness in baskets labeled "when I get" or "when ___ happens."

Just like us, the Israelites experienced heartbreak, and they also saw God come through for them in major ways. After leaving Egypt, they were in the wilderness on their way to the Promised Land to rebuild their lives. After being hurt, we are also on a journey to rebuild our lives. To comfort the Israelites, God gave them some specific instructions I believe are also for us:

Forget the former things; do not dwell on the past. See, I am doing a new thing! Now it springs up; do you not perceive it? I am making a way in the wilderness and streams in the wasteland. Isaiah 43:18-19 ESV

The "new thing" God did for the Israelites is happening right now for us. God's new thing is the process. It is not "happily ever after."

We often cannot perceive the "new thing" because we are looking for the new house: new car, new relationship, new circumstances or we are looking at the past. God's new thing is the process of change happening on the inside of us, as we become who He is calling us to be.

In addition to telling the Israelites He was "doing a new thing," He also promised to provide by "making a way in the wilderness and streams in the wasteland." Essentially, God is saying He will provide right now...while we are still in the wilderness. We just need to trust His provision.

Trusting God's provision sounds good, but when things do not go according to my plans, I feel an urge to do something. God distracted me from trying to control results and outcomes with my behavior to dancing towards obedience.

Instead of being focused on everything not meeting my expectations or pushing my happiness off until _____ happened, God called me to trust him with the results and be obedient.

What? Obedient? I was looking for change and happiness. What does obedience have to do with change and happiness? I can imagine God saying... "Good question!"

One devotional I used to study obedience challenged me with the following questions:

What is the last thing God told you to do? Who are the people God has placed in your care?

From those two questions, I asked myself: "Right now, how can I be faithful in what God has already told me to do?"

I wasn't sure what the last thing God told me to do was, but I was 100% sure about the people He placed in my care. God placed my children in my care. I was working in a physician's office. God placed my patients in my care.

I needed to be faithful in being Aryonna and Anaiya's mommy. My faithfulness in being the best mommy I could to them was NOT dependent on anyone else. I also needed to be the best Clinical Pharmacist to my patients.

One of my first steps in moving on with my life was to embrace being a single mom. I began to use the challenging moments with my daughters as opportunities to pray and talk about God's faithfulness. It was hard work, and it certainly took a village, but my girls did not miss out on any activities and thrived at school, with their friends, and at church while I was single and afterward.

At work, I concentrated on providing my patients with the best pharmaceutical care possible. I stopped wishing I was working somewhere else or that I was a wealthy princess who did not have to work. To my surprise, I began to experience peace at work.

I love this quote by Oswald Chambers from the My Utmost for His Highest devotional:

"If you obey God in the first thing He shows you, then He instantly opens up the next truth to you."

As I began to focus on who God placed in my care, I received direction on other things in my life. I also started to ask God what my next steps should be instead of using all my brain space for wishing things were different or incessantly trying to be "happy."

"Happiness is letting go of what you think your life is supposed to look like and celebrating it for everything that it is." Mandy Hale

Prayer:

Dear God,

Thank you for being a God who provides life-sustaining streams in the wastelands of our lives. Forgive us for not perceiving the new things You are continually doing. Help us move on with our lives by embracing obedience.

Amen

Dance Steps:

1. Write what was the last thing that God told you to do?

_____

_____

_____

_____

_____

_____

_____

2. Who are the people God has placed in your care?

_____

_____

_____

_____

_____

_____

3. How can you be faithful in what God has already told you to do, right now?

_____

_____

_____

_____

_____

_____

_____

Move On-Tell Your Story

JEFF AND I GOT MARRIED on a warm evening in July of 2017. Three months later, my church asked me to lead a Bible study for married women called *Becoming Mrs. Betterhalf* by Holly Furtick. I just about laughed out loud at being asked. Didn't they realize I had only been re-married for three months? How could I provide advice on marriage when I had been divorced?

I felt unqualified and worried about how women who had been happily married for years would feel about a leader who had been divorced and remarried for only three months. Despite my feelings, I prayerfully decided to lead the study.

Once the study began, I understood why God chose me. Instead of my story decreasing my credibility and making a mockery of my group, my story increased the welcoming atmosphere of our group. Our group was made up of women who had been married more than twenty years, women married for at least five years, women who were separated and at crossroads in their marriages, and we also had a young military wife who had only been married for two weeks!

My story of heartbreak, reconciliation, heartbreak again, separation, reconciliation, another heartbreak, separation, divorce after sixteen years of marriage, singleness, remarriage, then newlywed, allowed me to understand and empathize with every woman in the group. God showed me one of the most amazing connections we can make with others is in sharing our story.

Our small group of women, on all spectrums of marriage, shared stories and encouraged each other. Intertwined in each story were glimmers of God's comfort, care, saving grace, and redemption. We celebrated when one of the women who entered the group as separated, ended the study with a decision to reconcile her marriage. We consoled another woman who was also separated but concluded the study headed for divorce.

The age-old saying "misery loves company" contains quite a bit of truth. There is community in suffering. It is healing to the soul to hear someone who has been where we have and survived, say "things will get better." Personal pain can bless others, and it is actually part of God's design.

All praise to the God and Father of our Master, Jesus the Messiah! Father of all mercy! God of all healing counsel! He comes alongside us when we go through hard times, and before you know it, he brings us alongside someone else who is going through hard times so that we can be there for that person just as God was there for us. 2 Corinthians 1:3-4 (The Message)

The demographics of our group and the healing conversations that were shared helped me see my pain had a purpose. I did not go through all I went through for nothing. What I thought would surely be the end of me was actually an awakening into the woman God was and is calling me to be.

I have had the opportunity to pray for and with so many women in similar situations as mine. Sharing my story with honesty and vulnerability strengthens my resilience. Each time I share about my pain, I hear my story right along with my audience. Suffering is in my story but so is victory.

Suffering and victory are in your story as well.

Often, we get so busy living life we lose perspective on how far we have come. We remember how much it hurt, but we forget how just when we thought it was the end, God came through for us. One of the main ways God helps people is through other people. If we take the time to look back, we will see people along our paths who held our hands, were kind and met needs.

Disappointments are part of all of our lives. Some are small and easy to get over, and others demand a long time to bounce back from. Massive or minuscule, our hurts provide us with an opportunity to draw closer to God and other people. When we draw close to God, He draws close to us. When God is near, our rescue is a sure thing.

If you have ever been rescued, the world needs to hear your story.

Give thanks to the LORD, for he is good; his love endures forever.

Let the redeemed of the LORD tell their story—those he redeemed from the hand of the foe...Psalm 107:2 ESV

The process of being hurt, forgiving, being rescued, and moving on by telling our story is the distracted dance of resilience.

"Don't waste your pain, let God heal it, recycle it, utilize it and use it to bless other people,"–Rick Warren.

Prayer:

Dear God,

Thank you for rescuing us. Thank you for sending people in our lives at just the right time to comfort and care for us. Please forgive us for being shy about sharing our stories and for not seeing ourselves as people who were rescued and have something to share with the world. As we move forward, please keep us mindful of our stories and give us the motivation to use our pain to bless other people.

Amen.

Dance Step:
Write out your story. Include the pain, the lessons, the redemption, the setbacks, and your rescue.

_____

_____

_____

_____

_____

_____

_____

_____

_____

_____

_____

_____

_____

_____

_____

_____

_____

_____

_____

_____

_____

_____

_____

_____

_____

_____

_____

_____

_____

_____

_____

NOTES

1. Miller, Paul E. Beginning a Praying Life Navapress Pub Group, 2019.

2. Kasper, C. H. (n.d.). Our Daily Bread Experience. Retrieved September 9, 2018, from https://odb.org/2016/03/13/self-care/

3. Collins, J. C. (2001). Good to great. London: Random House Business.

4. Genesis 13 Commentary - Matthew Henry Commentary on the Whole Bible (Complete). (n.d.). Retrieved November 10, 2018, from https://www.biblestudytools.com/commentaries/matthew-henry-complete/genesis/13.html

5. 3. Erickson, M. (2016, January 18). Ruby Bridges' Ordinary Answer for an Extraordinary Problem. Retrieved from https://www.deseret-news.com/article/865645675/Ruby-Bridges-the-answer.html

6. Social support and ambulatory blood pressure: An examination of both receiving and giving. (2006, August 14). Retrieved January, 2019, from https://www.sciencedirect.com/science/article/abs/pii/S0167876006001917

7. OConnor, E. (1987). *Cry pain, cry hope: Thresholds to purpose.* Waco, TX: Word Books.

8. TerKeurst, L. (2012). *Unglued: Making wise choices in the midst of raw emotions.* Grand Rapids: Zondervan.

9. Chambers, O. (n.d.). Get your daily dose of wisdom. Retrieved from https://utmost.org/the-purpose-of-prayer

10. Warren, R. (n.d.). Never Waste Your Pain, Part 2. Retrieved from https://pastorrick.com/listen-online/never-waste-your-pain-part-2/

Suggested Songs:

Brown, Chris, Brock, Mack, Furtick, Steven, Joye Wade. (2017). O Come to the Altar [Elevation Worship]. On *Here as in Heaven* [Mp3 file]. Charlotte, NC: Elevation Worship.

Torwalt, Brian, Torwalt Katie. (2014). Holy Spirit [Francesca Battistelli]. On *If We're Honest* [Mp3 file]. Nashville, TN: Fervent Records.

Furtick, Steven, Ntlele, Matthews, Williams, Jane (2016) Yahweh [Elevation Worship] On *Here as in Heaven* [Mp3 file]. Charlotte, NC: Essential Worship

Mitchell, Vashawn, Feaster, Phillip, Gray, Lehman, Rodger, Calvin. (2012). Turing Around for Me [Vashawn Mitchell] On Created4This: Motown Gospel

Crocker, Matt, Houston Joel, Ligthelm Salomon. (2013) Oceans (Where Feet May Fail) [Christafari-Avion Blackman] On Anthems: Deluxe Lion of Zion Ent (2016)

Millard, Bart, Glover, Ben, Lewis, Crystal, Garcia, David, Timmons, Tim. (2017). Even If [MercyMe] On *Lifer*: Fair Trade Services

ABOUT THE AUTHOR

Katina Boyd is a Clinical Pharmacist, fitness entrepreneur, Bible study leader, and speaker. She leads hundreds of women to experience how the Word of God and the power of grace rejuvenates faith and enriches lives through her weekly fitness classes, blogs, and small groups. Those who know her best would tell you Katina is just a Jesus-loving working mom and wife who sometime struggles with managing a blended family, being over-scheduled, the never-ending cycle of laundry, and trying to be on time. Although the "struggle is real," Katina dances through her life with joy!

She lives with her family in Kernersville, North Carolina.

Connect with Katina, read blog posts, see family photos and follow her fitness and speaking schedules:

Website: www.katinajboyd.com
Social Media @KatinaJBoyd

Made in the USA
Columbia, SC
28 February 2019